From the Inside

From the Inside:

My Life As Bingo of the *Banana Splits*

by

Terence H. Winkless

BearManor Media

2020

From the Inside: My Life As Bingo of the Banana Splits

Published in the United States of America by:

BearManor Media

4700 Millenia Blvd.
Suite 175 PMB 90497
Orlando, FL 32839

bearmanormedia.com

Printed in the United States.

Typesetting and layout by John Teehan

ISBN—978-1-62933-564-3

This book is dedicated to my parents,
Ethel and Nelson,
and to my brother Jeff,
the greatest Fleagle imaginable.

Table of Contents

Preface

In the Summer of 2019, I received an email out of the blue asking me if I would be interested in participating in an autograph-signing nostalgia event as the guy who once portrayed Bingo the Gorilla on *The Banana Splits Adventure Hour*. The email was written by an industrious fellow and all-around good guy named Stuart Hersh who was coordinating any number of "celebrities," Barbi Benton among them, at the event. I know this because she was sitting at the neighboring table, an invitation I answered immediately. The invitation was not a complete surprise; an enterprising fellow in England named Mike Grant had created a Facebook page about the show, and for months I had been reading *Banana Splits* posts, and making comments myself, correcting errant assumptions, and generally parsing out information. Interest had indeed been simmering, and was headed for a boil.

It was resolutely impossible to say no to this personal appearance. The coordinators were supplying round trip airfare, nights at the Hilton Hotel in Parsippany, New Jersey, and per diem for food. Furthermore, Al Roker, who had been a fan of the show when he was a kid, got wind of our presence at the event and requested to interview us for *The Today Show*. What an astounding package of joy.

So it was, that the surviving members of the Banana Splits, Bingo, Drooper, and Snorky were reunited for the first time in fifty years, and for two and a half days signed autographs, took pictures, and shook hands. It was invigorating, entertaining, and surprisingly exhausting. Hayley Mills sat at a table next to ours and I got the chance to tell her how much I'd been her fan since *Tiger Bay* (1961), where she played a tomboy who befriends runaway seaman Horst Bucholz. I was surprised when she told me she hadn't heard from anyone else at the event how terrific she was in that film. I went on a fan-like exploration at one point and met the cast of *The Warriors* (1979), Walter Hill's classic fable about a gang trying to get back home after the truce/meeting they are attending is broken up by sinister forces. Michael Beck was happy to meet me, despite the fact that I'd turned down hiring him for a gig on *Pacific Blue* (1996) a television show I had directed—indeed, he'd been just plain too young for the part. James Remar thought I was there for an autograph from him, when in fact I was just there to commiserate about the loss of a guy I knew casually who had directed him in an award-winning short film; it was a little awkward. I visited *The Sopranos* (1999) room/booth and had the chance to tell "Furio" (Federico Castellucio) that he and I were parking our vehicles at the show-biz office building at 9000 W. Sunset once upon a time, that I had told him I was a fan, and that he had told me to screw off in no uncertain terms. I reminded him of this and we had a good laugh. Touring the tables and meeting people I'd long admired was as much fun as I've had as an adult in a very long time.

As a result of that nostalgia-show appearance, and the continually growing membership on Facebook's *Banana Splits* page, I realized I needed to sit down at the keyboard and recount everything I could remember that might be remotely amusing about shooting that show and my life during that time.

Introduction

I CAN HEAR THE KNOCK QUITE WELL, which is surprising because inside the big, thick orange Bingo costume it is never easy to hear anything at all, even the music pumped into the Hanna-Barbera sound stage to which we bop around in the videos. That extra volume should have been a hint that something was not quite right. I didn't exactly have time to acknowledge hints; I had a cue to react to, that is, when that knock comes, I'm supposed to answer the door. I galump my way toward it (Bingo the Gorilla didn't exactly move like a gorilla, or like a human being… he galumped from here to there, giving you the impression that he was some sort of beast.) Before I can get to the door, it flies open and slams against the wall of the set. In stalks 90 pounds of angry, real, live chimpanzee. Judy the Chimp. She's there to deliver a message that *Daktari* (1966) can be seen after our show on your local stations. In less than a second, she has crossed the ten feet separating us and now she's jumping six feet into the air trying to determine how to rip me apart. I turn and discover that Fleegle the Dog and Drooper the Lion (my brothers, inside the costumes) are both atop the podium that is part of the set. How they scaled the five-foot high podium I will never know, but there they are, holding on to each other and shaking as Laurel and

Hardy when some bully threatened them. By now, this screeching chimp has attached herself to my leg and no matter where I turn, there she is, snarling and making strange noises. (And, of course, apes are known to attack males in the testicles… all in all, it was very nervous-making.) The trainer had to come out and pry her off of me, and later, after the trainer had produced his pistol and shown it to Judy to calm her down, we are informed that Judy was infamous for having taken a big bite out of some actress, and that Judy has continued to work well past her five-year retirement date because she is so smart. Smart indeed. She certainly knew how to get the upper hand with the guys in the costumes. The ire and those teeth bared at me is an image I will never forget as long as I live. It spooks me out even now, fifty years later.

1

In the Beginning There Was a Rice Krispie

In June, 1968, I was attending college at Southern Illinois University in Carbondale, Illinois. It was not the only college that accepted me—I'd also been invited to attend Oklahoma City University, but Oklahoma didn't seem like me and instead of heading off in the fall like all of my friends, I decided to wait and go in the winter. It is among the best life decisions I've ever made. (A tad more detail: by statute an Illinois state school with SIU's charter had to accept any student if he waited a quarter before attending. It spoke to my terrible grades in high school.)

I drove my MGB home from college on a Friday and my mother announced to me and my younger brother (by 17 months) Danny, that our older brother Jeff was driving in from school in Ithaca, N.Y. and that we were all flying to Los Angeles in a couple days to try out for a kids' TV show that our dad was involved in. I imagine that a lot of young guys' reactions to this might have been sheer surprise, but we were fairly accustomed to stuff like this. Our whole lives we'd been on the edges of show business thanks to Dad's career as a creator of television commercials.

N. B. Winkless, Jr. (author's collection)

N. B. Winkless, Jr., my dad, had been a journalism major when he went to school at the University of Wisconsin in Madison, and had accepted a gig as a writer of advertisements for $25 a week for an outfit back east, called Remington, whose client list included Calso Gasoline. He'd made his way from one agency to the next, as guys in that world will do—he worked at Batton, Barton, Durston and Osborne, aka BBDO, also Needham, Louis, and Brorby, and wound up as a creative VP at the Leo Burnett Agency in Chicago. His clients there included some huge accounts, such as Marlboro and Parliament cigarettes, Sunkist, and Kellogg's cereals.

At that time, Kellogg's was big on creating cast commercials—there was *Dennis the Menace* (1959) featuring Jay North—*The Beverly Hillbillies* (1962) with Buddy Ebsen and Irene Ryan… Many of my dad's commercials were animated, from Charlie the Tuna, to Tony the Tiger. Perhaps the best, from my point of view, and maybe the best remembered is the Snap, Crackle, Pop, Rice Krispies jingle. The three-part harmony ad was widely lauded; and the musical parts were so much fun to sing that I taught them to class-mates and we'd sing them in the back of class to the consternation of more than one instructor.

Snap, what a happy sound,
Snap is the happiest sound I've found,
You may rap, tap, slap clap,
But Snap makes the world go 'round.
I say it's Crackle the crispy sound,
You gotta have crackle or the clock's not wound,
Geese cackle, feathers tickle, belts buckle, beets pickle,
But Crackle makes the world go 'round.
Now I insist that Pop's the sound,
The best is missed unless Pop's around,
You can't stop hoppin' when the cereal's poppin',
Pop makes the world go 'round.

In case you've wondered about the lyrics are, now you know them. The commercial is on the Internet if you're ever inclined to sing along with it. The animators for the Snap, Crackle, Pop jingle were former Disney guys who went on to create Quartet Films.

There was, however, a vast array of Hanna-Barbera characters pitching for other Kellogg's products, and since my dad was high on the Kellogg's advertising food chain, he got to know Hanna and Barbera quite well. These guys were all about the same age, had faced a lot of adversity in the Depression and WW II, and were now enjoying the fruits of their labors. Hanna and Barbera had started with just the two of them, along with Fred Quimby, doing *Tom and Jerry* (1954) for MGM, and by the 1960s had generated enough business that they had a grand three-storey building on Cahuenga Boulevard in Hollywood, a vast library of cartoon characters, some of whom had their own half-hour shows on network television—*The Huckleberry Hound Show* (1958) and *Hey There, It's Yogi Bear* (1964), in particular—and in 1968 they had sold a live action show to NBC: *The Banana Splits Adventure Hour* (1968). It was sort of a *Laugh-In* for kids, i.e. *Rowan and Martin's Laugh-In* (1967)—some of the details of that sale are part of Joe Barbera's biography, in which he describes pitching the show to Kellogg's and the NBC network by having one of his people, wearing a Yogi the Bear costume, burst into the room at a cue from Joe and sit in the lap of one the bigwigs (from Joe Barbera's autobiography "My Life in Toons" © 1994 Turner Publishing, Inc.) Joe Barbera was big on chutzpah, a word that quite rightly gets thrown around a lot in the film and television business.

This move into live action was daring and admirable; they were taking a risk far outside of their comfort zone. Animation, after all, is very controllable sort of undertaking. It requires vast amount of planning and vision—storyboards for days—but yo u're not likely to get rained out, and at the end of the day, a guy with a pencil and a pad of paper can create something that entertains people.

In order to achieve this rather huge step into live action production, Hanna and Barbera would need some athletic actors with an understanding of comic timing, of what the camera was doing, and who had tremendous stamina. To clarify, we didn't have comic training per se, merely lots of high school stage experience, and plenty of chutzpah of our own to make up for whatever we lacked formally.

My dad grasped early on the need for willing, capable, athletic actors to inhabit the suits, and he told Joe and Bill that he had just the guys for this task, namely my brothers and me. We were off and running.

2

Welcome To Your New Life In Hollywood of All Places

I ALWAYS SAY, "I packed a bag for three days, and I've been here ever since." It's not just me cynically cracking wise, though that wouldn't be outside my bailiwick. When we boarded the plane that took us west, I had no idea that I'd never go home again. It was thrilling and disconcerting, but mostly a buzz. The realization that you're never going to return to a place is something that comes along only gradually—as time passes and you don't return. The equation is mighty simple.

It was so long ago that American Airlines placed fresh packs of cigarettes on the seats to be smoked in-flight. Not whole packs, just the little three-in-a-pack numbers, a form of packaging I've never seen in retail. I've seen other forms of cigarettes sold. When I was in the Philippines directing my first martial arts movie, *Bloodfist,* in 1989, the street vendors would run out to the cars stopped at traffic lights and sell them individually. The traffic lights always took forever to change, probably realistically seven or eight minutes—it has always been my contention (well, since I was there in 1989, anyway) that the traffic lights were set deliberately long so that the poor folks could come out and sell their cigarettes, their hotel packets of shampoo and conditioner, their toothbrushes, and their mints, to those stuck at the traffic lights.

I am exaggerating, of course, but from my experiences in the Philippines I would put just about nothing past them. People lived in wooden crates under the docks, also in garbage dumps. The second floor of every hotel was a brothel. There is no middle class—you're either very poor or very rich, like the executive producer of *Bloodfist*, Cirio Santiago. Cirio was a cheerful enough kind of guy—and why not? His father had been a distributor of movies, and after he passed, Cirio had inherited not just the distribution business, but also a bunch of film-making equipment, including some archaic lights and a rack-over Mitchell. Big digression here: Back in the 40s, after sound had come in, there evolved a camera known as a Mitchell, or more precisely, the Mitchell BNC. The Mitchell BNC was the size and weight of a Volkswagen. BNC stands for "Blimped Newsreel Camera." (We shot with it on the Taal Volcano, which recently blew up.) Not only was it unwieldy, it was a rack-over; that is, what you saw through the view-finder was not what the lens of the camera was seeing the way that your garden-variety Sony Camcorder does. When I did my internship on *Soylent Green* (1973) the camera operator confided in me that he had frequent terrible nightmares about having the camera pointed in the wrong place because he had not accommodated what they call 'parallax;' that is, the discrepancy between what the camera saw and what the view-finder saw. I know, I know, it's way too technical to keep track of—I'm not technical at all, and my limited knowledge gets me bollixed up.

American Airlines flew the three of us to Los Angeles and our dad picked us up in his leased Mustang and we drove to Hollywood. Los Angeles is a little confusing in the way it's built. There's no direct way to get to Hollywood from the airport. It's northeast—and what you do is trudge north up the 405 then cut over on the 101 when you get to the San Fernando Valley. It's no big deal once you know your way around, but in the beginning, it was confusing as all get out. In 1968 downtown Hollywood was not as bedraggled as it feels today. It was the beginning of the hippie movement, some time before hippies were absolutely everywhere. There wasn't the sense of druggie desperation you experience as you walk down Hollywood Boulevard. There were, and are, other kinds of desperation. Many dreams got to the Left Coast and hit brick walls.

We encamped at a little motel my dad had frequented called the Hollywood Hawaiian located at approximately Yucca and Ivar. I say approximately because from the map I consulted to remind me of street names, I get the distinct sense that there's something new on that spot now.

We very quickly adapted to the modest time change. It was only a two-hour time difference—and what the heck—we were there to audition for a show on NBC, you bet we adjusted fast. For Jeff, my older brother, this was the logical correct course for his life. He'd done every imaginable production in high school at New Trier High School in Winnetka—he'd even been a director of the annual student-created production of Lagniappe, and had directed Ann-Margret Olsen before she became Ann-Margret. I had done my share of productions in high school, as had younger brother Danny, so Dad was clear-eyed in suggesting that we'd know what to do with these suits. We would find out what in short order.

The very next day, Dad delivered us out to Hanna-Barbera to meet Bill and Joe, and to walk across the street to Ruth St. Denis* dance studio to meet the costumes. In the process of committing this to paper it occurred to me to find out a little more about this woman whose name actually has an asterisk. Wikipedia states, in part "... she was at a drugstore with another member of Belasco's company in Buffalo, New York, when she saw a poster advertising Egyptian Deities cigarettes. The poster portrayed the Egyptian goddess Isis enthroned in a temple; this image captivated St. Denis* on the spot and inspired her to create dances that expressed the mysticism that the goddess's image conveyed. From then on, St. Denis* was immersed in Oriental philosophies." None of this relates directly to *The Banana Splits,* but it does speak to the millions of stories of people travelling to Hollywood to pursue their dreams, including us, though we didn't know to what extent when we met our alter-egos.

The costumes were lying in the middle of the room, still in their dry-cleaning bags. Lying on top of one another it was not easy to make anything of them other than their color. But it was quite a mountain of cloth, about four feet high and a 4x6 heaping rectangle. I'm not going to pretend that I can remember who took out which costume and put it on, but I can say that in just a few minutes we determined who would be which character: Danny became the lion because the costume was the tallest; Jeff took the green dog, maybe because it was a kind of chartreuse color that had always given him a hard time (all three of my brothers are color blind—that doesn't mean blind to color, it just means that the rods and cones in the retina get confused in the brown-green range—they don't know what color beige is. Green, tan, brown—it's all the same. Danny wanted to be a pilot for a couple minutes and I've always wondered if he'd have passed the FAA exam, which requires some ability to see colors.) With Danny taking the lanky one (Drooper), and Jeff taking the garish chartreuse one (Fleegle), that left me with the orange one, a gorilla named Bingo. Some have speculated that he was an orangutan, but despite that fact that he was orange, he was a gorilla. I know only by reading scripts at the time, which referred to Bingo this way. Being Bingo was perfect from my point of view; I was a gymnast, and swinging on vines in the jungle or swinging on rings in the gym it all seemed to fit together. I liked the huge grin and the snazzy green vest. He was character with a lot of character. And though it had been many years since I'd put my parents through the agony of my learning to play the drums, Bingo played the drums. A case might even be made for the idea that Bingo resembled Mickey Dolenz of *The Monkees*. Mickey also has a trademark big grin.

And yes, those of you who remember the show, and can count, know that there were four Banana Splits characters. The fourth was an elephant named Snorky; he was, I have read, a baby elephant, not that that ever really impacted anything. Snorky was not played by a brother (though in fact we have an oldest brother by the name of Nels, not an actor, a one-time film production manager, but a guy with no interest in being in the elephant suit.) Instead, Hanna-Barbera hired from within—they brought in a guy named Jimmy Dove from a different department that was not performance-oriented. Jimmy had his work cut out for him; he was wearing the least inherently personality-imbued costume; he was not related to anybody with any sway; and he was thrust in front of the camera straight off. It was not an easy task; I'm sure he always felt a little left out, but I've got to believe that no matter how difficult it was, it was a promotion from the Xerox room. Heck, man, it was show biz…!

Now that we knew who was who it was time to put the characters to work. We trundled down to Marina Del Rey so that we could board Bill Hanna's personal yacht, the Galatea, to shoot a "romp." These were essentially pre-MTV videos—in which the characters jumped around to pre-recorded music, and pretended to play the music with prop guitars, since we were ostensibly a rock band. There's every reason to believe that the Splits existed only because the music TV show *The Monkees* (1966) was a hit, since television likes to rip itself off at every opportunity. Of course, *The Monkees* existed only because the Beatles had done *A Hard Day's Night* two years prior in 1964. (Anytime I can connect what I did to the Beatles pleases me no end, and this will probably not be the last time I mention them.)

Though I'm quite sure the *Banana Splits* show had already been sold to NBC, you would not have known it by the way the earliest musical romps were created. This was very basic stuff—but surprisingly clever considering we were limited by just being on a boat. The image that comes to mind, and that is in a video that survives through today, early in 2020, is of Bingo (me) getting his foot caught in the rope of an anchor that's being hurled overboard, and I'm being dragged in by it. That illusion is very convincing and funny (though maybe a bit shocking to kids). We shot all of these segments on the not busy side of Catalina, the North side. Nineteen years later I would revisit the North side of Catalina, but that time it was as the director of my first movie, *The Nest* (1988), in which we sold Catalina as an island off the New England coast some place, some place very non-specific. (Making Southern California look like New England was an endless challenge in that picture. Every time you turned around, a palm tree or a Spanish-tiled roof would leap into the shot. In particular, in that movie, there's an establishing shot of a main character's house, and I must have looked through the camera a dozen times, and I never saw the palm tree, right there in the upper right quadrant of the shot. It was a real lesson in how the eye can be drawn where you want it to be drawn—mostly the center, especially back 1987 before people started shifting focus. Further, I wasn't alone in not seeing the palm tree; the gaffer (the guy who sets the lights) missed it, as did the Director of Photography. It wasn't until we got the material back in dailies the following day that anybody saw it. I'm not sure we saw it even then. Further, the shot is in the movie to this day. I recently revisited it on Amazon and thought it was pretty good, especially for a first effort.)

During that initial shoot we did most everything at Catalina on Bill Hanna's yacht, and there may have been a reason that we spent no time on shore, in addition to a shortage of permits, which I have no reason to believe we'd have had; the North side of Catalina was absolutely swimming, so to speak, in bird guano, at the risk of freaking out anybody. You could not take a step… maybe it was the time of year, maybe it was something else… but it was indeed something else. Memorable to this day in 2020. The photography we did was all done on the boat, not on Catalina itself.

My recollection is that Bill Hanna, Dan Ellithorpe and my dad were guys behind the camera. I have to say, Bill Hanna was one of the most generous, most friendly rich guys I've ever met. I always picture him with a genuine smile. He only occasionally came to the set; I believe that he had full faith that what was being shot was going to work. Joe Barbera was also a good guy, eager to treat us well and make sure we had what we needed as employees. He had a very a different style from Bill's—a sort of chutzpah-based cheer. Years later, my writing partner Alec and I got the plum gig of writing *The Jetsons* into a live action movie at Paramount. (It never got made; the studio did a budget which came out to twenty-one million, and they'd wanted to spend only twenty million. These days, of course, those numbers are ludicrously low.) But it gave me a chance to reconnect with Joe Barbera who came to a meeting or two, and remind him that I'd once been in the Bingo suit. He was gracious and forthcoming, and asked about my dad, who was still around I was able to report.

Next, we were off to San Francisco. We jumped onto a Pacific Southwest Airlines flight (a local carrier no longer around) and 40 minutes later we were in what's still my favorite city, me and everybody else. I still get a major high just thinking about it. After all, only a couple weeks before I'd been concerned with passing my exams in my fifth quarter at Southern Illinois University, and now here I was in this amazing, vivid city with its spectacular views and architecture.

We were in San Francisco for only three days. We hit the streets running. The guy steering us literally into the streets was an Egyptian cameraman named Fouad Said. Fouad was fearless, and a great example for me as a budding film-maker. I can see him throwing himself into the street, on his back, 16mm Arriflex camera affixed to his eye, and gesturing for us to cavort around in front of him. Or to jump over the camera. Or to ignore the oncoming traffic and keep cavorting. "Make a lot of noise, guys!" he would shout, which made no sense at the time, but anything that kept up the energy is what mattered.

Fouad had been the Director of Photography on the location shoots for *I Spy* (1965) with Robert Culp and Bill Cosby, back when you could mention the latter's name without raising eyebrows. It was out of the process of shooting that show that he would go on to develop the Cinemobile which developed his bank account into the zillions. (As I write this and go on-line to check out stuff, I discover that Fouad went to USC at the same time I did and actually graduated after I did. Surprising people appeared like that a lot at USC. I remember seeing Eric Burdon [of the Animals] one day at the film department. I never saw him in a class. Another day I ran into Steve Reed with whom I'd grown up in Kenilworth, IL. and had worked at the post office. It was very peculiar.

We shot a lot of footage at Fisherman's Wharf with people gawking at the brightly colored beasts playing off the curb as if they owned the streets. It was unusual at the time to see gaudy colored characters like us out and about, even in as wild an environment as San Francisco. Since it was still very early on in the process there was no system developed yet for keeping us going. This fatigue concept will come up any number of times; it was extremely grueling work. My costume and Fleegle's costume, which we wore under the lights on stage weighed about 45 pounds and were made from 4-inch-long shag carpeting. The head pieces had articulated mouths which could be opened and closed by pressing down on a padded piece of metal under the jaw. It was not a very accurate process, almost impossible to open your mouth to keep up with speech.

The voices of the characters were not our own; they were prerecorded and we moved our mouths in sync as much we could with what we were hearing. Bingo was voiced by long-time voice man Daws Butler, Fleegle by the great Paul Winchell (also a fabulous ventriloquist and famous for voicing Tigger in *Winnie the Pooh,*), and Drooper by comic actor Alan Melvin, who had been a long-time member of *The Phil Silvers Show* aka *Sgt. Bilko* (1955) and Alice's boyfriend on *The Brady Bunch* (1969).

For the outdoor shooting stuff, we were provided lighter costumes—40 lbs.—without articulated mouths, but in the hot sun in Dallas and Cincinnati that five-pound decrease made no difference at all. I'll get into more specifics later when we get to shooting on the stage, but suffice it to say, in the early going especially, little had been designed to acknowledge and treat the amount of heat generated inside the suits.

What we did that first weekend was cavort on the streets as long as we could and then leap aboard an Econoline van that accompanied us. The Screen Actors Guild has very strict guidelines about how actors are to be treated. It's a powerful union and there's no use thinking you can make a film without cooperating with them. You can make your film without union actors, but it's not likely to be very good. We weren't yet members of Screen Actors Guild (SAG); it was several weeks into shooting the first season that the subject came up with the production manager, a cheerful guy named Clark Paylow—great name for a guy whose job is hiring people. For no particular reason that I'm aware of, the subject came up one day when we were three weeks into shooting. "You fellows are in SAG, right?" We told him we weren't. All the blood drained from Clark's face and he ran off to make some calls about it. I've been in and out of SAG ever since, never having actively pursued a career as an actor as my brother Jeff did. I imagine if I had I would never have let it lapse. In the end, Clark Paylow arranged for us to pay the hefty entry fee into SAG, thus making us and the company in compliance with the master union arrangement that oversees, or tries to oversee, all productions in California.

On that weekend of shooting in San Francisco the company violated every SAG rule imaginable that did not include vehicles. You mean it's against the rules to have the actors dance around in the street in costumes in which they can hardly see? You mean they're not allowed to run alongside their production van and jump in while it's moving? You mean having them dance in the street without a cop directing traffic is not allowed? Write us a letter and we'll take it under advisement. Of course, it was Dad who was responsible for a lot of the early production stuff, and he was known to have thumbed his nose at any number of restrictions-rules-guidelines. I should know; I'm his son and I'm a great deal like him, both in temperament and wit.

Despite having no system in place yet to relieve the flagging actors, we got some mighty handsome material including some great stuff at Coit Tower. Drooper and Bingo both looking under Fleegle's ears to see what he sees as he's looking through one of those coin-operated telescopes. Our niece, Danielle Winkless, aged five, can be seen holding Snorky's trunk as she walks along the ledge under the Tower. There was also some amusing stuff as we battled gravity on Lombard Street. At a certain point, however, brother Dan got hit with the flu, or mere exhaustion, and adman Dan Ellithorpe had to take his place in the suit briefly. It's the only time I'm aware of in which a non-real actor, so to speak, was in the suit for something that went on the air.

In fact, though, the best was yet to come, and that was crossing the Golden Gate Bridge in costume. The company had rented a convertible: a Chevy Impala, brand new of course. We reconnoitered on the south side, agreed that we'd stay 20 feet or so behind the Econoline van which Fouad was shooting from, and off we went. Jeff was driving inside the Fleagle costume. Jimmy Dove as Snorky rode beside him. Danny and I sat in back UP on top of the closed canvas roof, with our feet down on the seats. Even as I write this, I can see the moving violations flying off the page.

Everything went fine while shooting on the bridge. It was a beautiful sunny day in June, before the usual grim of a San Francisco July kicked in—SF is famous for being cold in July (baseball announcers are always carping about it.) We had gone across a couple of times, but on the last time north across the bridge, just before we wrapped for the day, the California Highway Patrol pulled us over;

well, he pulled over Jeff—but not for the big, peculiar chartreuse head he'd been wearing only moments before, but because Drooper and Bingo had been sitting atop the closed roof. He didn't mention the head, didn't ticket Jeff for driving with an unlicensed gorilla and lion, or a floppy elephant. He let Jeff off with a warning and went on his way. I'd like to believe that the charm of the costumes and the characters they represented would get us off the hook even today.

3

So This Is Hollywood

We had been living initially in a motel on Highland Avenue in Hollywood—it was called the Hollywood Highlander—and one night we came back to our rooms after an exhausting day of shooting. And we were locked out. Our dad hadn't got around to paying the bill—it wasn't a question of having the money—our dad simply hadn't received a bill asking for payment and he'd been working all day on the show, as we were. As to being locked out, Dad was, to put it mildly, short-tempered—his language when he read the desk clerk the riot act, was especially colorful, since he was a professionally creative guy. He'd have made a sailor blush, as the phrase goes. Thus, with a couple of phone calls we shuttled off to a place my dad had stayed at often during his many trips to LA to shoot/supervise commercials: the Hollywood Hawaiian. This motel was right in downtown Hollywood. It too had a pool. Better yet, it was right next door to a Cantonese Chinese place, which served Moo Goo Gai Pan which was to die for. The first time that Jeff, Danny, and I ate there we ordered enough food for three families, let alone three guys. It was delish.

We were living in the Hollywood Hawaiian—up in town, but we were shooting down in the western flats on Pico west of Robertson, at a little sound stage called Carthay (in what really just felt like a converted garage), so it was a haul. (As I write this, I keep looking things up to see what's what—upon Googling Carthay Stage I get Carthay Studios and it tells me that the Grateful Dead recorded there. I'm not surprised—years later when I was editing one of the films I directed for Julie Corman, *The Westing Game*, Fleetwood Mac rented out one of the sound stages and blasted the heck out of everybody on the little lot on Main Street in Venice. It was great, being a Fleetwood fan.)

We were shooting "down in the flats"—that's anything that's not in the hills, and represents the way you discuss how to get some place in Los Angeles—"down in the flats"—"on Olympic, west of the 405." "On Sunset out past Will Rogers Park." Yes, of course there are numbers, but you have to zero in on what part of town in a somewhat general sense. "Hollywood—a few doors down from Musso and Frank's." Anybody who's been in town for more than a few months knows where all these locations are because they have been used as markers for other places. Back in the day—before there were cell phones and GPS devices—there was the Thomas Guide—a telephone book-thick catalogue of every street in LA County, or whatever county for which you bought it.

No move to Los Angeles is complete without the ritual of securing a car. I went out and bought a new racing green MGB. Danny bought a Mustang, and Jeff got his little yellow VW hatchback out from Illinois. I know that what people drove fifty years ago is fairly worthless, but LA makes you rethink that, like it or not. What you drive is who you are to a certain extent. I once talked an actress I didn't know very well into going out with me. She was unsure about me until I guided her to my car; she didn't care about the car except that it happened to be the same kind she drove. (Okay, it was an Alfa-Romeo. By far the worst car I ever owned. Needed to replace the fuel filter every six weeks or it quit right there on the spot. I moved from it to Japanese cars after that—vowed never to go back.) The point is—you can't talk about LA without mentioning cars. I am positive I will mention one again later.

I am aware that I was extremely lucky to be buying a new car, especially at that age. I was nineteen years old, and that car was one of two that I bought with the *Banana Splits* money. There was the MGB, and later, when I was deep into making films at USC, a Dodge Van with a V8. We worked hard and we were paid well. SAG minimum at the time was in the ballpark of $600 a week, with a buy-out later on when the show went into reruns; a buyout is a lump sum of money, instead of weekly check; it's more efficient for the company and the money is about the same to the recipient.

Looking back, regarding this actress, I should have shoved off the minute I learned she drove an Alfa-Romeo. They are sexy cars, but they belong to a style of life I learned much later in Bulgaria:"обичам да **ми** е трудно," "I like it the hard way." It's a philosophy that suggests that life's lessons are had only by arriving at them through difficult moments, which I have to say, has a lot of merit. There were some Greeks who felt that way too, and there's probably a whole school of them even if I can't recall USC's Dr. Kevin Robb's teaching on the matter just now.

Life at the Hollywood Hawaiian was okay. It had a pool which we exploited every night—actually, there were a couple things we did virtually every night. The main one was eat. The work inside the costumes was exceedingly laborious. Literally exhausting—as in, using up of resources. A shooting day in any Hollywood production is always at least twelve hours. (When you're shooting in town it's a twelve-hour day and a five-day week. When you're out of town, it's a twelve-hour day and a six-day week. Though on the foreign shoots I've worked on in Bulgaria, *The Berlin Conspiracy* (1992); India, *Goreyan Nu Daffa Karo* (2014) and the Philippines, *Bloodfist* (1990) the producer contracts for a six-day week, but he's lucky if he gets ten hour a day from the crew. They don't mind Saturdays so much, but Sunday, forget about it.)

Being inside the suit truly tapped you out. Imagine—you get to work at 6:30 am. You go to your dressing room and find your costume. You put on the first T-shirt of the day. You pull the company jumpsuit on over the T-shirt and your underwear and now you go out and link up with the wardrobe person, in this case, Judy Savalas, or one of her crew. She hands you your 40 pounds of orange shag carpeting which is your Bingo costume, and your foot and half long gorilla feet, and off you go to the set. Sometimes we rehearsed only in the jumpsuit, but to get a feel for what we were up against in terms of moving around the set, it was often better to be in the suit, minus the head. This would permit you to see where you were going during rehearsal, and try to commit the space to memory. Rehearsals were only approximate. The set was built as a proscenium, that is, like a stage play; there is no fourth wall. It's the way that virtually all sit-coms are done. People talk about "breaking the fourth wall," which means talking to the camera, since the camera, after all is where the fourth wall would be… if there were a fourth wall.

The set wasn't a huge space, maybe ten feet by twenty-five, but when you're accustomed to having 100% of your vision and suddenly you're cut down to 45%, you start counting on other senses that hadn't ever been brought into play.

The most egregious example of this for me goes as follows: one of the big, entertaining aspects of our show, and one that everybody remembers when thinking back on the show, were the Banana Buggies, or more properly, the Amphicats. This was a six-wheeled vehicle that we drove primarily in the opening credits of the show, but also in various music romps. The things had a top end of only about 30mph, thank the great cosmic Fudd (as my philosophy professor called him), but they were incredibly unstable. They weighed 218 kg, according to Google (which means 480 lbs.). They were steered by pulling back on the left stick to go left, and right to go right—but they had no real brakes. To stop you simply powered down. Good luck stopping on a dime.

Thus, as with all vehicles when being photographed by a movie camera, the idea was to go as fast as you could [safely] go. Let's be honest here—there were always brackets around the word "safely." Nobody really cared if you were safe as long as you were going fast, or looked as if you were going fast. Stuff racing past in the foreground is a handy trick for creating the illusion of speed. James Cameron is a master of this (I hasten to add that Cameron is also a graduate of the Roger Corman School of Filmmaking; he got his start working for Corman in the art department.) In the first *The Terminator,* they couldn't get the car to go backwards fast enough with the stuntman, or Schwarzenegger, riding on the hood. Cameron had the car back up against a fake wall and moved the wall in the opposite direction to heighten the speed. Worked darn well, didn't it? I know only because I watch those "Making of…" shows to see what tricks I might steal myself . . . my best gag is in my film *Ladykiller* in 1996 aka *Scene of the Crime,* in which I had the main character, played by Ben Gazzara, replays for himself, that is, flashes back to the incident that killed his partner, which I did by moving Ben's desk out to the place where the incident happened, so that it appears he's at his desk, but then when he remembers the event, he steps right into his flashback which is in a park setting. It was very cool. (*Ladykiller* was about the grizzled cop who teams with an actor to solve the murder of co-eds. It co-starred the very talented, fine actor Alex McArthur.)

There were no illusions applied in making the Banana Buggies go fast. You simply jammed the thing into forward and held on for dear life. This was fine when we were out in open spaces, or at the Rose Bowl where there were no impediments. We did a whole bunch of stuff out in the sticks in the San Fernando Valley. We're not talking about the section of the San Fernando Valley where Bob Hope lived in Toluca Lake, which is next door to Burbank, and very verdant and nice. We're talking way out deep, where even the housing developments hadn't reached yet. We were way up in the hills, dry and dusty and hot, of course. This area was not scouted very well—it was too vast. So then, my job was to go as fast as I could over the rough terrain—it always looked cool to see us bouncing in the Banana Buggies—and I ran head-long into a Cyclone fence because I simply couldn't see it. The costume's weight and thickness played a happy part in that event because it prevented me from breaking any bones. This was the same location where the thing tipped over on me while I was making a tight turn, and, despite its weight, my adrenaline shot me to my feet and threw the thing aside, like the old wives' tales one hears about mothers lifting cars off their kids, though not so extreme… what's 480 pounds among friends? Yes, shooting out on location was always a thrill. It was at this same out-in-the-woods venue that I got stuck up a tree in my Bingo costume and suddenly I saw the crew scramble away because a rattlesnake had appeared. Ah, what fun…

Looking back, and now with some producing experience under my belt, I have to wonder why we weren't replaced with stuntmen on those days, for some of this location stuff? Why did the actual actors have to risk life and limb when nobody could see their faces, I wonder…? It's true that getting into the costume that I had sweated up would have been a drag for a stuntman, but those guys are tough and they could have handled it.

I recall only two times that other people were in the suits when we were shooting the show—the time Danny got sick when we were shooting at Coit Tower, and the time that some extras, who were hired by SAG contract to be on set for lighting purposes, put on the costumes ever so briefly, and just once.

4

So This Is Texas

A WHOLE BUNCH OF THE MATERIAL in the opening titles of the show was shot at Six Flags Over Texas in Dallas. It was June of 1968. I'd never been to Texas, let alone in the summer—in a gorilla costume. It was unimaginably hot. Yes, I know I talk about heat a lot. It is the leitmotif here, if the descriptions of being a gorilla in a TV show can have a leitmotif. It was so pervasive that it forced you to consider which way to die is better—from heat, or by freezing to death. My conclusion was that freezing to death was better. Mind you, I was only 19 and 20 years old while doing the show, so the mere fact that I was debating which way to die is disconcerting if you ask me.

Despite the amount of sweat we produced, great care was taken to keep the costumes photographable. This was not often easy because my brothers and I were quite hard on them—what mattered to all was getting something lively and often funny on film, and if that meant falling down and spraining an ankle or ripping an orange arm loose from a Bingo costume, so be it. And no, despite the amount of sweat pouring forth, the costume did not stink; the actual costume was protected from the human beings, and vice-versa by virtue of the jumpsuits we wore. Like insulation on a house.

Somewhere during the first season, after we repeatedly had complained about the astonishingly brutal heat—not that the heat was in doubt; all anybody had to do was look at us after a take when we took off our heads and see the sweat dripping in buckets—NASA was contacted. Yes, *that* NASA was contacted to see if there was anything they could do to resolve the problem. They came up with a system that was ingenious in a way; if you froze a CO2 cartridge and then popped it into a little fan device connected to a rubber hose which was attached to your head, it would blow cold air on you. Just one major problem: the fan device and cartridge lived in a little package which was strapped onto your body over your kidneys. On a TV show in which the characters acted like children and thus fell down often, this was completely impractical. Despite their fine intent we wound up blowing through hoses and humming. They became the world's most expensive kazoos.

Another thing I have to say about working in the suit, besides sweating, is the extent to which your appetite builds. It was phenomenal. In Los Angeles we went often to a place in the Los Feliz section of Los Angeles called Michael's. It was your basic upscale steak joint, fairly elegant—so it was a little odd to find these three bedraggled looking kids come in and scarf down steak and lobster like it was going out of style. Never an inch of fat accumulated. I'm still a lightweight. Jeff was always slender, as was Danny. We ate a lot of calories; we expended a lot of calories. It was the late 60s, so yes, we all smoked. It was stupid; we ignored the package warnings and the requests from my mother to quit. I know I dwell on this; it's a cautionary refrain. If I could go back in time and never take them up I would. I did finally quit, some twenty-five years ago, about five years before my daughter, Lara Terry Winkless, was born, which was quite deliberate on my part; I quit so I could be around longer for her.

The Six Flags bits incorporated a bunch of local talent; that is, kids swarming the colorful characters as we walked around the park. This seemed to happen around every corner—but the crew simultaneously brushed them off of touching us and recruited them to be on camera with us. The Texans were generous and smiley—lots of smiles, that "Y'all come on back real soon, ya hear?" kind of thing, but genuine, and they really meant it. The drinking age was lower in Texas than Illinois and California at the time, so I had the "pleasure" of ordering a potent Manhattan without really understanding what it was. I knew its name, knew it was an adult drink—man, and how. It's a mixture of bourbon or rye with sweet vermouth and bitters. It's heavy. I was never a big drinker, just beer as a kid, nothing at all these days (I quit completely about a year ago when I noticed it was interfering with my sleep.) That Manhattan really kicked my butt. I had experimented with it just because I was in state in the union during the production where I could try it at that age. Haven't had another since.

In the costumes we did a whole bunch of stuff with the miniature train they had there, where we are alternately steering the train then running after it on foot. I really have no sense of who was directing that material; I tend to think it was a fellow named Tom Boutross who did most of the romp stuff if there was a director at all. The romps counted so much on their editing, their mise-en-scene, so that they hardly needed directors. They were shaped and timed by what the editor did in the cutting room. There's a shot in the romp shot at Six Flags Over Texas that has always driven me crazy; it's a shot of my brother Danny in a roller coaster and the tail of his Drooper costume is flying loosely off of his suit. The reason it drives me nuts is that I always think that his tail might have been caught in the tracks of the roller coaster and might have dragged him over the side of the coaster car and under the tracks. Ah, yes… what if the Wolf **had** come out of the woods, to riff on Prokofiev's "Peter and the Wolf."

One of the editors on the show was a fellow by the name of Warner Leighton. Warner was a terrific guy, another dedicated smoker, so he's in the past tense. He had been a guy who assembled cartoons in-house at Hanna-Barbera; he really learned his way around an editing room, or cutting room as it's known, particularly using a device called a Moviola. A Moviola is an old-fashioned editing machine in which the picture is run through a gate on the right side, and the sound is run on the left. Sometimes there would be three heads on a Moviola so that you could have dialogue on one track, music on a second track, and the picture on the third, and really get the sense of what the movie would feel like. (Of course, this kind of thinking is archaic these days. Digital film-making has made Moviolas, and Steenbecks utterly obsolete, though what remains is the debate over whether or not learning to edit with film makes one a better editor. We'll never know. Does writing with a pen make you a better writer than if you're working on a computer? Not in my case. My hand cramps up and I cannot write by hand at all. I doubt I could sustain much working on a typewriter.)

Warner was very much active when in the Fall of 1974, following the series, he took me on as an assistant. It was a real mercy hire because I had almost no skills as an editor and even fewer as an assistant. I was, however, hungry and eager to learn, and Warner, as I say, was a great guy. Always willing to crack a smile no matter how much pressure was on. Among the projects he was editing, in addition to a constant stream of commercials of all sorts, was a western called *Shootout in a One Dog Town* (1974), a western directed by Burt Kennedy, with a great cast, including Richard Crenna, Stephanie Powers, Jack Elam, and Dub Taylor of *Bonnie and Clyde* fame. I had to deliver something to Dub out somewhere deep in the San Fernando Valley, an ADR script or something, and he made me guess how old he was. He was in his late 60s at the time and I'm pretty sure he wanted me to guess a lower number. Being only 25 myself I had no idea how ridiculous my guess of 47 was. I think he wanted me to say something in the 50s, but at my age then I didn't know that game. I know it now, you can bet, and play it every chance I get. Like Dub, I look younger than I am, or not.

The real coup de grâce of working for Warner had been dribbling in for weeks, only I didn't see it right away. That is, I didn't grasp what it might turn into for me. The late H.B. Halicki, aka Toby, had been dealing junked cars from his multi-acre lot of them down in a real beauty spot, Gardena, California, between the 110 freeway and the 405 freeway. You could not walk outside without hearing the highway, though there are lots of spots like that in Los Angeles. My wife will tell you that it *all* sounds like a freeway. One day, and I don't know what lit his fuse, he decided he'd make a movie using these acres of junked cars. Toby had vision, there's no question about it. We'd had *Vanishing Point* (1971) and *Dirty Mary and Crazy Larry* (1974) and it's not as if America had ever fallen out of love with its cars. Los Angeles was designed and built on the notion that people would live out in the 'burbs and drive in to work. That rather backfired, but the love affair didn't wane. Thus, it was, when Toby decided to make his film, he was catching the last moment you could do it. He actually started around the time that gasoline rationing first started in Los Angeles… that was a horrible time.) Toby looked that mess in the eye and said screw it, I'm going to make *Gone in Sixty Seconds*—the original, not the remake with Nicholas Cage.

Each week somebody would show up with some footage of cars for which I would have the task of syncing up the footage (that is, making the sound and the picture run together so that lips are moving at the right rate with what somebody is saying, or so that "whack" sound of a hammer coincides with the picture of the hammer striking.) There were cars being stolen, cars being wrecked, cars being taken apart. Okay, says I, these guys work in a chop shop. They steal cars, take the pieces off and part them out, or change the VIN number and recycle them back onto the street. Okay, those are the bones of a car-stealing movie. Then one day a dialogue scene came in… much easier to synch up, but really a horribly acted and written scene. To be fair, I had/have the feeling that the "actors" were just making up their stuff based on a notion of what the scene was about. This is something that skilled actors can do really well, but these were the guys who worked in Toby's shop taking cars apart for a living for real. When Toby needed an insurance adjuster for a scene, he called his friend the insurance adjuster, who literally could not walk and talk at the same time, not while the camera was on him at any rate.

I watched a bunch of this dialogue stuff come in and I asked Toby what the set up was for it all. He said they hadn't really worked that out yet. Which was pretty astonishing. We had I- don't-know-how-many minutes of film and they hadn't worked out what the set up was or how it would be conveyed. I made him a proposition; if I wrote some scenes that connected it all together, would he let me direct the scenes that I wrote? That sounded okay to him. He was a guy who drove cars, worked hard, partied hard, not a guy who sat at a keyboard caressing dialogue or working through intricate scenes. He did let me direct the scenes that I wrote (after a fashion) and I learned you can't make a silk purse from a sow's ear, and you can't get insurance adjusters to do Ben Kingsley even if the guy looked a little like him. Where did I get off? What kind of qualifications did I have that I should ask Toby for the right to direct those scenes? Stay tuned, I'll get there.

5

Welcome To the Movie Urge

Back in Evanston, Illinois, in that splendid, fateful summer of 1968, I hooked up with some guys home for the summer from school, or merely still home having not gone to school. One of these guys was a fellow named John Byrum aka Jake. I don't think we ever knew each other in high school but for some reason he knew a guy I'd been in a band with, Mark Miller—though these days that's more properly Dr. Mark Crispin Miller, Professor of Communications at NYU. Byrum, and Nick Cleland, and Dave Cleland, (no relation), Flip Bimstein, and Bill Musham and a bunch of us got together, a bunch of times to play touch football on the Village Green in Hubbard Woods, in the north part of Winnetka, Illinois. (I get chills just writing that. There really was a village green.) Hubbard Woods had some really snooty shops in addition to a Village Green, and a couple of restaurants, including Hubbard's Cupboard and a deli that was the junior version of the one in Highland Park just up the road apiece.

Byrum is a guy who's always had people revolving around him. He's like a planet with his own moons and stars; there is gravitational pull about him. He's as gregarious a human being as I've ever known. Oh, you don't know that guy? says Jake, here, I'll introduce you. Oh, you know him? Hell no, says Jake, but that shouldn't stop us. He is utterly fearless. I've come to believe he was emulating Neal Cassady to a certain extent, about whom he made a movie—*Heart Beat* (1980), in which I appeared briefly. I will elucidate:

The movie was a toast to the Beat Generation of the late 50s. In part, about the three-way relationship among Cassady, Jack Kerouac, and Carolyn Cassady, and the inability of middle America to accept a new kind of art and style of people. (That doesn't do it justice, but this is my story, not Jake's, and he'll just have to understand.)

Nick Nolte, playing Neal Cassady, comes into a bar where he used to drink in San Francisco, but since everything has changed as a result of the book written by his pal Kerouac, Neal can't get a beer in his favorite pop-stand as he'd call it. It's now a Beatnik coffee house where people read poetry and appreciative audience members snap their fingers in response instead of applauding—it's all just agonizingly hip, which is Byrum's point. The irony is that it was Kerouac's writing about Neal that has made it impossible for Neal now to get a beer. A rich, painful irony. Nolte as Cassady plunks himself down next to me, already at the bar, and orders a beer. The Bartender explains that it's just soda-pop and coffee these days, but winds up introducing me, aka "Youth in Bar," to the Cassady/Nolte character. The Bartender tells me I'm in the presence of greatness; that is, Dean Moriarty (Kerouac's name for Cassady in *On the Road*) and I'm all gaga. I turn to him and say, "Dean Moriarty, you mean the cat from "On the Road? Hey, man, you got any boo?" He looks at me like I'm a reptile. I continue. "You know, tea, pot, marijuana." He shakes his head and shoves off. "Dean Moriarty, my ass," I say, "the guy doesn't even know what boo is." Because I've asked him this, however, an undercover cop at the bar gets on to him and changes the course of his life… which meant that the scene could not be cut out, which was great for me, but a drag for Byrum and his editor, Eric Jenkins. Jenkins told me later that they had to use every lower-your-voice-filter they had in the post production house in order to dial down my shaking timbre. Indeed, I'd been nervous as it gets—it's not as if I'd ever really been an actor; what little I'd done had been inside a gorilla costume or in film school, both very non-threatening environments.

Further, I hadn't had a chance to see the script or anything. Jake told me my dialogue upon arriving at the set, which is far from the way it's normally done. "Normally" they send you the scene a couple days before and you can study it. Make each syllable your own. What the heck, I was doing a favor for a friend because the original guy, another old friend of Jake's (and a guy I was friendly with, too, from the touch football games and home in Winnetka, Nick Cleland, was unable to do it at the last moment for some reason. On top of that, the Director of Photography was the famous Hungarian New Waver Laszlo Kovacs who demanded to know of Byrum why his old dependable friend, me, was screwing up so much. I had the feeling that there had been other conflicts between them and I was just being added onto the pile of crimes. When you watch it today you wonder what the problem was. Ah, the magic of movies, and I still collect about twenty bucks a year in residuals.

In addition to playing some regular touch football games and the attendant beer drinking parties in the evening there was an event that happened only once—maybe twice—that really got my attention. A guy Jake knew named Bob Greenberg had an apartment down in Evanston. I have no idea how they knew each other—maybe from Southern Illinois University where all of the reprobates went at one time or another apparently (me, Jake, Nick, maybe Greenberg). A whole bunch of us went down to Greenberg's apartment in Evanston (which by itself felt racy to me at 19 years old—this guy had his own apartment? Wow…) Greenberg was a film buff and collector, and the night I went along he screened two memorable things: the Alfred Hitchcock classic *North by Northwest*

(1959) and a pornographic cartoon called *Eveready Harton*. What blew my mind, in addition to a pornographic cartoon from 1929 (say what?), was the mere fact of screening a movie in somebody's living room.

I mean, of course, my family and I had been watching movies in our living room forever, but they were always commercials or home movies of vacations, like water skiing in Wisconsin. The idea of watching full Hollywood-made movies in the living room—this was something completely astonishing. The many forms of movie viewing at home we have been through since then makes this seems absurd, but back then it was too cool for school. In fact, by the summer of '68, I had just taken one class at Southern Illinois University that might be relevant to what was dawning inside me. It was a class about making newsreels. My assignment had been to do a thirty second piece on whatever we chose as a subject. I chose the controversial subject of owning a vehicle, which was allowed only if a student was living a certain distance from campus. I created a story about a guy who lived in Giant City State Park and had to race many miles to get to school. It told an amusing story but it ran about a minute and ten seconds. All fine and good, but the assignment had been to make something thirty seconds long. The instructor gave me an A for the effort and a C for ignoring the restrictions. Still, this mere one-minute epic had lit my fuse—when that met the event(s) at Greenberg's, well, I was propelled toward something, but first there was this costume to deal with.

Image Section

Bingo.

Bingo in Banana Buggy.

Bingo leaves his feet to play.

Bingo relates a story about something.

Drooper.

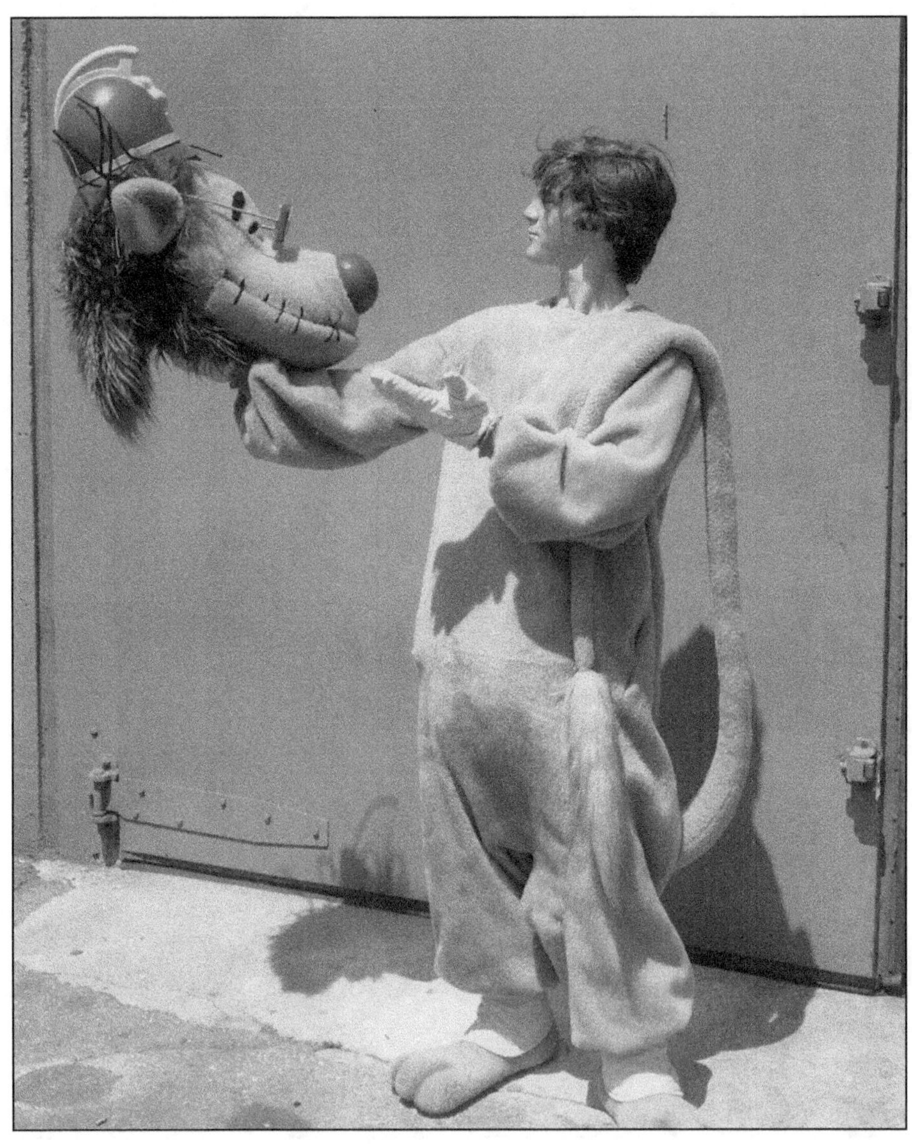

Dan Winkless plays Shakespeare.

Drooper bows.

Drooper falls down.

Drooper with guitar.

Early Splits, where are Bingo's sunglasses posing in front of HB headquarters.

Genuine Splits in the costumes.

Other people in the costumes.

Other people in the suits—Bingo would never hold a cymbal like that.

Other people in the suits.

Super Drooper flies in.

T H W CU SANS HEAD.

Terence Winkless, left, Dan Winkless across, Jeff in BG, Jimmy Dove , right.

Terence, Jeff, Dan Winkless with back to camera, Jimmy Dove facing us.

The gang wonders what happened to Snorky.

The guys in action.

6

Winning the Rose Bowl

ONE OF THE ROMPS/VIDEOS we did that first year was shot at Southern California's famous Rose Bowl. It's astounding to look at it now. Using a bluesy number, *Soul*, by Al Kooper or Gene Pitney or Barry White, all of whom did songs for the show, the costumed Banana Splits drive the stuffing out of their Banana Buggies all over the field and all around the outside of the famous sports arena. It's surprising to me that they let us do this. We're whipping around their world-famous grass and ripping it up like crazy – but no worse than a USC game on a rainy Saturday I guess. Danny drove his buggy fast enough that it threatened to flip over but he caught it on time to right it. We played soccer with a huge beach ball a yard and a half in diameter. It was kitschy and cute and funny, but at the end of the day none of the music really made any sense for the nature of the romps, except for the Tra-La-La song which was the opening credits of the show. As to that, I might as well get into this now, so here goes…

My dad wrote the music behind the opening credits, that is, the famous "Tra-La-La" song which everyone knows and identifies immediately as the *Banana Splits*.theme song. I have read on line that composers Ritchie Adams and Mark Barkan wrote the song, but this is just plain wrong. I believe that Adams and Barkan had an overall deal whereby they were credited with the song, but they did not write it. This happens sometimes in TV land where everyone is vying for credit because with credit comes money and, in some cases, credit means future employment. In no uncertain terms, the Tra-La-La song was written by my dad on the slightly out of tune upright piano in our living room in Kenilworth, Illinois. (Hanna and Barbera attached their names as creators of all studio output, rarely crediting the actual artists who designed or created their characters.)

Dad was nobody's idea of a great composer; he knew how to play about six chords on the piano, but those chords served him well. He wrote the Good Morning song with them—Good Morning Good Morning, the best to you each morning – K-E-double L–O double good, Kellogg's best to you". He wrote commercial jingles for Charlie the Tuna, and Swanson's TV dinners, also for Marlboro and Parliament, also the coup de grâce which I mentioned earlier, the Snap, Crackle, Pop song which he wrote with brother Jeff's help and with the inspiration from Tinhorn's Lament from the musical *Guys and Dolls.* When you listen to the Tra-La-La song more closely you realize it's really just a riff on "Mama's Little Baby Loves Shortnin' Bread," (a plantation song) one step removed. (Along the same line of discussion, people on-line think that Bob Marley's Buffalo Soldiers is an awful lot like the Tra-La-La song; well, if it is, it's because Bob heard the Splits' theme a lot and it sneaked into his head, as the Splits came along in 1968 and Buffalo Soldiers wasn't written until 1984. A lot of Dad's songs were one step removed from something else; I always considered that to be a great strength and very clever. It made the client comfortable because he was hearing something familiar in a way, but not exactly a rip off, and when the client is comfortable, things are good.

Call it serendipity, call it dumb luck, but whatever you call it, for some reason the gods were with me, because even before I got word that I was going to be a Banana Split I had applied to the University of Southern California, I had somehow got it in to my head that I wanted to be a film-maker, and unlike Southern Illinois, with its one course in film-making, USC had dozens. You could study to be a writer, a cinematographer, a director, whatever you wanted to study – there was certainly no guarantee that you'd work in the field you studied, but you could indeed study it (indeed, we were warned in our first class that 95% of us would never work in the movie business—I have no idea what the actual stats are, but I can think of only a handful of people from my class who have worked in the business.) Part of what turned the tide for me was seeing *Doctor Zhivago* (1965) on the big screen when it was almost brand new.

Towns like Carbondale, Illinois got movies later than their big city counterparts, like Chicago, which meant that in the winter of 1967 it was a first-run showing at the theater on State Street in downtown Carbondale, a two-block long collection of old shops and restaurants, and one theater. In I wandered; I can't say why; I mean, I'd always loved movies—but to go by myself in the middle of the day was not something I normally did. *Zhivago* struck me like an out of control skier on the expert slope. The epic adventure, the beauty of Julie Christie, the sorrowful eyes of Omar Sharif. I was utterly blown away. It's the screening of that as much as anything else that got me onto track of wanting to make movies, though I didn't quite know it yet. I knew to the extent that I applied to USC because of the catalog I looked at in the SIU library, but I hadn't really put the two together.

I knew I wanted to make films, *Doctor Zhivago* had shown me that, or maybe I was just moved by Julie Christie, but whatever it was, it was irresistible. Thus it was that I went off to USC with its zillions of courses. I arrived at USC just after George Lucas and

John Milius had left, though Lucas's energy was still in the building. In the shadow of the multi-storey Girls' Dorm, the building was actually a former stables that had been repurposed to be the cinema department, which was kind of cool. It was a gray collection of one-story buildings that opened up onto a courtyard. There was a big room that passed as a stage. There was a long skinny room where the camera equipment lived. There was another room that housed a sea of Moviolas. There was an animation department. The cool thing though, was the courtyard. It was a great way to run into people, or to get to know people that you didn't know yet. There was an informality to it that made it work. All movie business meetings should be held in the courtyard; there'd be less pressure to produce decisions. The old cinema department is long since gone, replaced by a slew of slick buildings funded by Lucas and Steven Spielberg, though I don't know why Spielberg since he didn't go to school there, but he's certainly to be admired even more for donating dough to a place he didn't attend.

Along with a more casual physical environment back in the day, the entry demands were also less rigorous. A fellow named Dave Johnson was the guy in the big gym with whom you signed up. He was a guy whose bark was much bigger than his bite who gave you a grilling before he signed you up for anything in the department. These days, as I understand it, you need to have a letter signed in blood from your Senator. Back then all you needed to do was persuade Dave Johnson that you had ideas and energy and you wanted to implement them. Which fit me to a T, though I wasn't yet sure what my ideas were.

It was, however, an era where you could not be sentient and not have feelings about what was going on. The Viet Nam War was operating on eight cylinders and every day there were news reports about how many were dead and wounded over there, and how many protests on how many college campuses over here. Turbulence was the order of the day. The lottery system was initiated in 1969. My number was 202… the lottery took guys up to number 198. I don't know what would have happened if it had gone higher. If it had gone higher then certainly being the guy inside the Bingo costume was not going to gain me any quarter with the Army. All you could do was do your thing and hope for the best.

I arrived at USC at a kind of lucky time. It was before everybody and his sister was trying to make movies. Long before videos existed. Eons before there was a camera in your cell phone (what the heck is a cell phone?) Long before the digital revolution; you photographed and edited your films using film. A bunch of guys who went to school with are a lot more famous than I am. *Halloween* (1978)'s John Carpenter was a classmate of mine (also a roommate), as was Nick Castle of *August Rush* (2007); Robert Zemeckis (*Back to the Future* (1985) came right after us. It was an environment that gave you a rough idea of what it was you were up against in terms of the vast amount of creativity you'd be competing with. At that, it was only a mere suggestion of the level of competition. In one of the earliest classes you'd make a film and show it in class; and then people would criticize it. A lot of people couldn't separate the criticism of their three-minute movie from criticism of themselves—the late Dan O'Bannon was a particularly vicious and funny critic in these early sessions. It was a useful exercise in a business that is cut-throat to the max.

7

100% Upside

There is no question that the money I was making as a Banana Split influenced what I did as a student film-maker. Money always influences art, I learned, whether we like it or not. For me, what that meant is that I didn't shoot my films on 8mm or Super 8mm, like the rest of my classmates. I shot on 16mm, in large part because my dad had bought a little studio up in the San Francisco Bay Area. The studio came with an Arriflex camera, a Moviola, a Nagra sound recorder and microphone, a recording booth and a couple little editing bays. There was a certain amount of tussle between my dad and me in that he wanted me to move north and work with him at the studio. I was of two minds. Like every twenty-year-old I wanted to carve my own path—never mind that I was doing it with money provided by my dad's connections. In the end he realized that I'd be a better, more independent individual if I did it on my own, and he became my number one fan and advocate. When I graduated from college, he gave me a dictionary as a gift with the inscription: "To our son, the scriptmaker, just pick out the words and put 'em in order." As I say, being a wise-guy runs in the family.

Writing this all down certainly makes me see that there was only one path I was going to be taking. I was not going to be a banker, or diplomat, or a guy who curates art. I was going to be in the film business, like it or not. What's not to like? Never being sure where the next job was going to be coming from, or with it where the next dollar was coming from was no reason to dislike the entire business. Anybody who's ever had a whiff of it will tell you it gets into your bones. Under your skin. Then you're stuck. Forever looking for that next gig and always believing it will be the one that makes you financially independent. Be that as it may, I wouldn't have it any other way, not that I have any choice. The minute I donned the Bingo costume I was a goner. I'm a goner to this day. I have a job shooting later this year that is a sequel to the movie I co-starred in in India a few years back. Alec Lorimore and I have another project we're trying to launch.

I have been very lucky. I have had a total of two straight (non-show biz) jobs my entire life. The first was as a dishwasher in the employees' cafeteria at Marshall Field's at the Old Orchard shopping mecca in Skokie, Illinois. This was the kind of job a 17-year-old could get immediately upon graduating high school, and I did take a shot at it. The job consisted of gathering up dirty dishes from the tables in the employees' cafeteria, loading them into a fifteen-foot-long machine, retrieving them from the machine and placing them on trays to be put back into rotation. Not rocket science.

My co-workers were a couple of lifers, a man and a woman, who took one look at the wet behind my ears and knew they could get away with murder; that is, they could start slacking off. This started with them doing only part of their work and graduated to long, long breaks. They would go off for an hour at a time when they were supposed to be working. For me, it culminated with my taking my lunch break at my appointed time, and then, while I was eating, noticing that the conveyor belt was too stacked up to accept any more plates and dishes. Like a good kid, I got up from my lunch and started to clean it up. I was most of the way through sponging up the mess when I stopped and realized that it wouldn't have happened if my co-workers had been responsible enough to show up for their jobs. I left the mess, went and told the woman who'd hired me that I was quitting and never looked back. I spent the rest of the summer water-skiing behind my girlfriend's boat.

My other straight job was right after that summer of water-skiing. Having qualified for no college I wanted to go to, I spent three months waiting by working at the Winnetka Post Office. I totally loved this job; it was a great gig for an 18-year-old filling time before he went to school; the only jobs I'd had previous to the P.O. had paid a buck an hour. This paid minimum wage which was about $2.40 per hour back then. My initial job was as a sorter, a guy who "threw mail" into the slots where it would go in the suburbs. I was a sorter because I wasn't yet old enough to drive the mail vehicles. Being a sorter had its perks; Bob Schoenberger (the same guy I filmed sleeping in Giant City State Park) showed me where the free samples of diet pills were, and they made it possible to work the night shift. A guy who'd grown up in Kenilworth and was a touch older, Steve Reed, joined the mail throwers, and we had our own little band of brothers. I turned 18 and the job got more amusing. I took their driving exam, which a rhesus monkey could have passed, and this qualified me to drive the mail trucks. Because Winnetka has the huge houses with the vast lawns, a lot of mail boxes are those country-style mailboxes out next to the road, instead of ones that are right at your front door. The country-style mailboxes meant that the mail trucks had to be those right-hand drive stand-up numbers on which the accelerator was a lever operated by your toe, instead of a pedal. Great fun. Really slow.

When I went back to do the job in the summer after my first two quarters at school, I really got a dose of the trucks. I went to work at 7 am—way too early for an 18-year-old looking to have fun. I was assigned the special deliveries, and I had two hours to achieve getting them delivered. Thing is, I knew my way around really well, and even though the trucks were slow, I could work fast. I could get it done in only one hour, which meant that I could catch up on my sleep for an hour. I was rarely hassled by dogs as a mailman, just enough for the events to be really memorable. Lassie once bit me in the wallet.

Another time, I was made into a mailman sandwich by taking refuge behind a screen door to protect myself from a dog outside, only to be harassed by a dog inside causing me to pull the main door to me—as I say, mailman sandwich. Eventually, the outside dog took a hike and I was able to set my mailbag down in the closet. This allowed me to quickly dash outside, leap up to the second-floor gutter and pull myself up and enter the house where I called my supervisor, Bill Burmeister. I expected to get chewed out but he just laughed and laughed. He came out and rescued me and would have explained to the homeowner that my actions were innocent, but the homeowner was not around. Didn't have to be with that mailman-eating dog.

The coup de grâce of my dog events was not Lassie but some unmemorable canine who came growling at me out of nowhere—the stories of dogs and mailmen are real; they don't like having their territory invaded—so this dog flies at me from around a bush, and I notice a shiny object down in my bag (not *my* bag really, I was just temping) and I look closer. It's mace. I quickly read the instructions; they're not as complicated as stereo instructions—basically spray and stand back. I spray it at the dog and he yips off into the distance. He came back again, and this time all I had to do was show it to him and off he went.

Dogs notwithstanding, I really liked that job. Even so, there was a slight suggestion of show biz to come. My rescuing supervisor, a cheerful pudgy fellow, that same Bill Burmeister, recognized that I had a square jaw and a theatrical bent and he predicted that I would go to Hollywood. It was the summer of 1967; I had no thoughts, designs, or ideas about doing any such thing; he just shook his head and told me I'd be going. Maybe he had a clue thanks to a previous Winnetka Post Office employee, Rock Hudson. He'd had pretty much the same job I had, but old Roy Scherer's path was a very different path from mine.

I truly expected that I'd be back at the Post Office the following summer after college. Indeed, why not; I was good at it, the money was goodish, and I thought it was fun. Killer combo. I was wrong, however, about returning to the Winnetka Post Office, though I clearly have fondness for my time there.

8

It Was the 60s

Instead of the post office and Winnetka, it was off to California. What a time. It was *the* place to be. There's some discussion that it all started back east, but it's a short discussion. It all started at Berkeley. Not for me, I was nowhere near Berkeley, but that was protest central and that attitude filtered down to Los Angeles. The Splits paid no attention to all that tension.

We were a fun-loving colorful distraction to all that turmoil. There is a peculiar nod to the psychedelic times we were going through; some of the visual effects applied to both the cartoon stuff and the live action stuff on the show was designed to emulate psychedelia. The guys in post-production at Hanna-Barbera were hip and they were out to prove it. They animated very trippy elements into what we did. Some of this was achieved by putting us on a green screen stage. That is, one of the ways special effects are achieved is to put characters, whether it's the Banana Splits, or James Bond, on a stage with a green or blue background, and then electronically insert different backgrounds. A different, laborious version of this was used often by Alfred Hitchcock who used a process called rear-screen projection. E.g., characters drive a car on a stage and the mountain road is inserted behind them. By photographing us on a green (or blue) screen stage, we could be put anywhere, and any number of things could be put in the picture with us—a bunch of the videos have this process at work, see *Toy Piano.*

No sooner had we started shooting the show before we were finished for that first year. Six weeks goes by quickly, and in fact, six weeks to shoot an entire season of a show is unimaginable. This was achievable only because there was much more in the show than just the live action Banana Splits. There were also the animated *Three Musketeers* and *Arabian Nights*, and also the live action *Danger Island*. For the live action stuff, they brought in a young guy named Richard Donner. Long before *Superman* and *Lethal Weapon*, he'd directed *Zane Grey Theater* and *Wanted: Dead or Alive*, and *Have Gun Will Travel*, all really first-rate credits. Through some miracle they got him for this dinky section of a Saturday morning kids show. I have the feeling that the miracle was good money; not that there was anything foul about doing our show, but it was clearly a detour for a guy whose career was soon to take off. I have been advised that upon meeting Donner one of us, Danny, I believe, cracked wise and said, in the style of The Beatles in *A Hard Day's Night*: "So, this is the famous Dick Donner," a la George Harrison saying, "So, this is the famous Scotland Yard."

One of the wiser decisions made about *The Banana Splits Adventure Hour* was the decision to shoot the live action character stuff with three cameras. A wide shot (the whole set), a medium shot (maybe two characters), and a tight shot (a single character). This was good because it meant the guys in the suits—my brothers and me—didn't have to do the same action over and over again. This is no big deal when you have characters who are not wearing forty pounds of carpeting; but when you do, it is a fine brand of wisdom. It saved us a lot of anguish. It also got a little funky. We needed a close up of a character's hand pounding the gavel on the podium that sat on the set to call the club to order. Thus, Donner photographed the gavel being pounded—but shot it with three cameras, two of which were useless because they showed a headless character or a prop man. It was an odd indulgence, and it has stuck with me for all these years. Maybe I knew I was going to go on and make films for people who would very much want me to be more efficient than that (Roger and Julie Corman), or maybe anybody can see what a waste it is to shoot the prop man full body when all you want is his costumed hand on the gavel.

Donner had a supremely laid-back style with us—he had to. Though the shows were scripted, so much of it spontaneous that he never really quite knew what was going to happen. It wasn't as if he could storyboard it all out and then have us realize his vision. Donner's ability to go with the flow and embrace the impromptu nature of it all was one of his great strengths.

Indeed, Donner vaulted way past our show and into some of the biggest movies ever with *Superman* (1978) and *Lethal Weapon* (1987). He was/is a terrifically generous guy with a tremendous laugh. Nothing got you to perform more rambunctiously than a guy with a big laugh on the other side of the camera. It was colossal encouragement to keep doing what we were doing. Years later I ran into Donner on the Warner Brothers lot where I had an office with my writing partner, Alec Lorimore, and I reminded Donner of our association, and what hot fun we had on the show. He wished me well and laughed hard and went off to make another zillion dollars. One last Donner thing before I move on. Back in the late 60s he ran with Peter Lawford and Sammy Davis, Jr. and that whole Rat Pack crowd. As such, he owned part of a night club down on Robertson, just south of Santa Monica, called the Factory (probably because it had once been a factory—*clever....*) and, at our request, Donner went out of his way to leave passes for my brothers and me there. I saw Raquel Welch there, but she had a date and we moved on, but the gesture by Donner was appreciated.

The show's production generated an interesting collection of folks. In addition to the wet behind the ears stars of the show in the costumes, i.e. Jeff and Danny and myself, you had a long-time Hollywood first assistant director named Al Kraus—contrary to popular understanding it is the first A.D. who calls for quiet on the set, not the director. The director does the creative stuff, but the A.D. is the guy who gets the crew to do the work. Al Kraus did *Mission: Impossible* (1968*)* as well as *Gunsmoke* (1955) and *The Wild Wild West* (1966). The Director of Photography that first year was Winton Hoch who won three Academy Awards, for John Ford's *She Wore A Yellow Ribbon* (1949), for Victor Fleming's *Joan of Arc* (1948) with Ingrid Bergman, and *The Quiet Man* (1953) directed by John Ford and starring John Wayne. The second year's assistant director was Gary Grillo, a guy whose family I'd get to know later in a bizarre way—his brother married my ex-girlfriend Beverly—ah, Hollywood. Our costume supervisor, whose task never ended trying to keep the beasts looking good was a woman named Judy Savalas whose connection to Telly I could not say. The writing credits included Joe Ruby and Ken Spears who would go on to create their own cartoon manufacturing plant Ruby/Spears, which generated *Scooby-Doo Where Are You* (1969) among others. For that matter, the costumes themselves were made by some guys who wound up with stars in the Hollywood Walk of Fame, maybe the most famous kid costumes designers ever, Sid and Marty Krofft, creators of *Land of the Lost* (1974) among other things.

Back in the grounded world of going to college at USC, I was in my initial film-making class, called 290. Over the course of the semester we were to make six films. My first film was about the hippie who needed a match, and the non-hippie guy needed a smoke, and how they solved each other's problems. The second one was something about an apple and my pal Lorimore; the third one was about a straight guy who wanted to act like a hippie (lots of identity questioning stuff at work); the fourth is a mystery to me; the fifth was about a guy (my late friend Phil Dressler) who runs around San Francisco chased by a chaser who turns out to be himself. I'm pretty sure that the instructors, Woody Omens, Mel Sloan and Gerry Maguire were not going to recommend me to go on to the next level of instruction year until I turned in my great opus, *The Race Problem* (1968).

I'd been enamored of stop motion photography, i.e., having a thing move by photographing it two frames here, [push it along] two more frames [push it along], etc. so that when it's played back at normal speed, 24 frames per second, it looks as if it's moving by itself across the floor. I had a three-section little epic: 1). I animated a pair of mannequin arms, one painted with a hammer and sickle, the other painted like an American flag, so that they arm-wrestled and ultimately blew up everything 2). I put my younger brother Danny and his pal Randy in the street and had them race and crash until my old buddy John Nemerovski came along and drove them away as an ambulance, and 3). I took some children's blocks with which I spelled out White, Black, Brown, and Yellow with White trying to force the other colors down. In the end they all break apart and spell new words. I'm not sure what my conservative parents thought of this liberal streak in their number three son, but they didn't seem to mind. The film did well; it was purchased by Universal for their program of films by student film-makers; the LA Times gave it a splendid review in their assessment of the recent USC created films. The *LA Times* review read [in part] as follows: "One of the most imaginative entries was Terence Winkless' "The Race Problem," a clever bit of animation that manages to say a great deal about modern life with wit and economy..." It was sent to the Edinburgh Film Festival by the late Herb Kasauer as one of USC's entries in the festival there in the summer of 1969. I was lucky enough to travel there to see it play. It was a memorable trip; on an Icelandic Air flight, which stopped in Reykjavik to refuel. I sat next to a photographer from Milan who had been in Florida for the moon shot which had just taken place.

This guy had not showered for days. Yes, 17 hours next to this smelly photographer; if I hadn't been a nice kid of twenty, I would have asked for a different seat or my money back, but I didn't know then that you could ask for such things.

My first year at USC I lived a little apartment off of Jefferson on 32nd street. The van I had bought got robbed a couple times thanks to the neighborhood were we in. I'm quite sure that the apartment building is no longer there because when I visited a couple years ago, I discovered that even the street isn't there any more. USC expanded its boundaries and now what used to be 32nd Street is some kind of University housing. This was a bummer to me as I had met one of my oldest friends there, Alec Lorimore; I had needed somebody to pose with an apple for a very early film project at USC; it was the beginning of a beautiful friendship as they say in the movies. When I got back from Europe, I decided I didn't want to be robbed any more and that it'd be more fun to live in one of the gigantic houses that were near campus. USC had been built in 1889 at a time when downtown was the rich section of town; that changed over the years, and by the time I got there it was a white island in a black sea, not that I cared—I'm the guy who made *The Race Problem*, but I was ready for a change. Thus, I gathered together two of the guys who had lived in the former building with me, Bob Blank (and later his girlfriend Cathy Summers), and Art Bess, combined them with another guy I knew from New Trier Township High School, Winnetka, Illinois, Phil Dressler, and yet another from New Trier, John Gunthorp, and the five of us rented a big old mansion at 2627 Menlo Avenue. It was a splendid house: fifteen rooms, three bathrooms, two kitchens, a huge wide stairway, a ballroom on the third floor. We each had two rooms. It was great for parties, for shooting films, for whatever you needed a gigantic house for.

There was a dark element which we learned about some time after we had moved in. On the third floor, right off the ballroom there was what looked like a cage. We used it for storing luggage, but there were clearly some bars on the swinging door opening. In the Fall of 1969 as the Manson trial was getting underway, a reporter tracked down information that suggested somebody peripheral to the Family had lived in the house. The reporter came by and I gave him a tour of the house; the bars on the door of the luggage closet were all he needed to conclude that evil things happened here, and he was bound and determined to get me to admit that those were bars on the door of the storage closet. Heck no, those aren't bars, I said, knowing full well they were bars. Also, there was some iconography on the wall and some words I only just now looked up: Ordo Templi Orientis, which is purported to be a Satanic cult with a wide-ranging membership, from Stanley Kubrick to Paul McCartney to James Franco (who, by the way, got his first gig from me on *Pacific Blue*, and was the son of Doug Franco a classmate of mine who had gone to New Trier H.S.), and way back when, Charlie Manson. Make of that what you will; I refused to have anything to do with it then and I've probably said too much now.

9

Carry On, Fellas

There was one significant change in the midst of everything—a personnel change –Jimmy Dove's Snorky gave way to Bobby Towers' Snorky. Bobby was a real actor, had been recruited after playing Snoopy off-Broadway (to Gary Burghoff's Charlie Brown), maybe off-off-Broadway in another state, because I saw him perform as Snoopy at the Ivar Theater in Hollywood. Bobby actually came aboard only a matter of weeks after we started. Indeed, Jimmy had been installed in the costume primarily because he was the right size for it and had a convivial attitude about it all. You had to have a good attitude or you were toast. Also, to be more accurate (the tumblers click into place slowly after this many years), Bobby took over the part the first year when we returned to Los Angeles from shooting the romp in San Francisco.

What little I know about Jimmy Dove comes from the Facebook *Banana Splits* page. He is sadly no longer with us, and apparently harbored some resentment at the way he was treated. He thought the brothers Winkless were better accepted. He may have been right; I really couldn't say. I'm quite sure that Bobby Towers never felt that way. In fact, Jeff and Bobby were very good friends over the years. There were some alterations applied to the Snorky costume to allow Bobby to find ways to enliven Snorky, and he made the most of them.

As for the status of the costumes, many times people have asked me if "I still have my Bingo costume?" The answer is a resounding no. The costumes could barely be kept together enough to shoot while getting constant daily attention, so it's hard to imagine that they could endured for the fifty years since the show.

Each character had three costumes. Two were for shooting on the stage, and the third was for shooting exterior material—the romps. The difference was that the exterior/romp costumes were modestly lighter, and the heads did not have the articulated mouths. That was a huge difference in weight; it made it possible for me to do cartwheels in my Bingo costume without my head coming off. There is at least one scene that was used in which my head flies off, but it's very fast and the rest of the action takes the viewer's eyes away from headless Bingo.

The Snorky costume received some revision at a certain point so that he became a more string-ey version of itself. That point was between seasons on and two. Its inhabitant, Bobby Towers tells me that the newer version was less fringe-like, and easier to navigate in, but that some fans think the older version of the little beast was cuter

The other very memorable change in the production the second year is that we were no longer shooting in the non-studio environment of the Carthay Stage, but instead had found studio space at Golden West Studios up on Sunset. It was a whole lot better than driving down to the flats to Carthay (the former car garage.) Golden West was a genuine studio sound stage. It really felt as if you were in the movie business, or at any rate, the TV business. Little did I realize that it would be my last real studio and stage in a lifetime in the movie/TV business. Even *Pacific Blue* (1996), the TV show I directed for five years, shot on a stage that was a repurposed something else. I believe the only times I directed things on stages that were not repurposed from something else were on stages out of Los Angeles—in San Diego for *18 Wheels of Justice* (2000), and in Sofia, Bulgaria for *The Berlin Conspiracy* (1992). In Sofia we had neither enough lights nor enough heat. You could see your breath while shooting indoors. Brutal.

One of the cool upsides in shooting *The Banana Splits* at a studio instead of at Carthay, the converted garage/stage in the flats, was the sense of home that a studio cultivates. Anyway, I made it my home. I had a Dodge van at the time (the second car bought with *Banana Splits* earnings) It was great for hauling around film-making equipment, something I was doing decisively; I also used it to go out for fun in the evening and instead of going home and having to drive to work the next day, I used to drive the van to the studio, and talk my way past the guards by explaining that I was there to work the next day, and would park next to the stage, and go to sleep in the back of the van where I had a mattress and a little fridge. I'd never survive that today—get up and get going without hot water? Are you kidding me…?

Before we arrived for Season Two of the *Banana Splits* in 1969, we had the winter to enjoy. I was in my second year at USC, continuing to make films, and to pay for it all, we learned, happily, that there would be a second season of the Splits, and to promote it, well in advance, we were invited to host the New Year's Rose Parade Show in Pasadena, since it was an NBC broadcast, and as such, cross-promotion. We were not in the massive parade itself, just the events preceding it. The parade started at 8am, so this was even before that. Like 7am. I was never a big drinker, but at 20, I did like to party, particularly on New Year's Eve. Bingo was never more bleary-eyed than on that New Year's Day. Somehow, we got through it and I lived to tell the tale.

Richard Donner did not return for Season Two; a guy named Tom Boutross was hired to direct. Boutross was a former film editor with a backstory in low-budget films including *The Hideous*

Sun Demon (1958), according to the Internet Movie Database, or IMDb. Tom was a journeyman director; a guy who'd never make it big, or as my DP pal Bob Hayes might describe him, there was a certain quality he lacked, "the quality a guy who directs a pilot has is like the guy who can find fire for the rest of the cavemen when their fire has gone out," though he has a far more elegant way of expressing it. He'd get the job done, and do it on time, just not with any particular flair. He was far more dour than Donner had been, not that we really needed anybody laughing on the crew. We knew what we were doing and how to do it. We weren't exactly driving the show, but the fact that nothing ever quite went the way anybody expected it to meant that the film-makers had to stand back and let the colorful animals go nuts—the nature of the show, which leads to a short discussion of a technical aspect of the show.

Different film stocks have different speeds. Back in 1968 and 69, 16mm film was quite slow, about 25 ASA. By comparison, the show I directed for five seasons, *Pacific Blue* used a 16mm film stock with 400 ASA, very fast. The faster the film stock, the greater latitude there is in focus, the easier it is to keep a character in focus; the faster the stock, therefore, equals less time spent on rehearsals, equals less time spent overall; and in the film business you're always fighting the clock.

The speed of the film relative to shooting our show was this: we went forward to the camera and away from the camera constantly. It was important, as it always is, to keep us in focus. And since nobody ever quite knew where were going to be, the depth of field (the area in which we'd be in focus) had to be increased. The way to increase the depth of field, and thereby keep us in focus, therefore, was to increase the amount of light. The greater the light, the greater the heat, of course. The greater the amount of light, the greater the heat. You knew it was coming back to heat. It always comes back to heat. Whenever I think about being Bingo, I remember being hot. Hotter than I was shooting a film in Death Valley when it was 125 degrees.

The single best aspect of Season Two for me was irrelevant to the filming process; it was that it provided me the money to go to Europe. Instead, I did what every kid my age did at the time—I went to Europe at the first opportunity. I did not emulate my pal Byrum who had taken his tuition money for NYU and used it to go to Europe. I looked him up outside London while I was there, and we, and Barb Hannon, jumped in my VW beetle to go to Greece; the car broke in [what was then] Yugoslavia and we all had to hitchhike back to England, but that's another set of stories; if we do a second edition I'll plug them in then.

I seem to have been destined one way or another to have something to do with Eastern of Europe, if my VW wasn't breaking there in 1969, then I was assigned to go there in 1991 to make a film called "The Day the Wall Came Down" but released as *The Berlin Conspiracy*. The movie was about the CIA operative (Marc Singer) assigned to work with the STASI operative (Stephen Davies) to stop the cannisters of evil nerve agent from getting into the hands of terrorists. We shot in Berlin for about a week, then did the rest in Bulgaria, where Corman had signed a deal to make a series of pictures. This was the Corman way—find a place with experienced crews and lots of equipment, dive in and make a deal, then send a director he figured could navigate the territory and hack the strangeness of it all to deliver a movie. I did it for him twice, once in the Philippines, and again in Bulgaria.

This place was utterly flabbergasting. The Soviets had only just left, but the imprint they left behind would take many years to wear off. For example, there was no commercial advertising of any kind—not on television or on billboards. You paid all your bills at the central post office. All hot water came from one source. There were practically no streetlights, I've never been to a darker place at night. On my initial visit there, no condiments were available, because people were hoarding until prices evened out in the European Union, And yet there was a genuine charm about the place. People sitting parks on a summer evening. Nothing manufactured. If you went to dine at a place called "the Old House" it was named that because the structure was 500 years old.

The film I made was pretty good—terrific technical credits, and excellent performances out Singer and his counterpart, a role I cast with my old buddy Stephen Davies. I ran out of English speakers on that film, however, and I played a pretty big part. I'll admit, it lit my fuse to do more acting. While I was editing that one, I was recruited to be in Jim Loftus's *Trade Routes* (1994) on which I learned the best acting lesson I ever had from an actor in the picture, William Hope, who advised me, "Act slowly. Whatever you do, take your time. If the director wants it faster, he'll tell you, Until then, take your… time."

To finish my thought about shooting in Bulgaria on a high note; whether the film was any good or not is judgment call, but there no doubt that making it changed my life: I met my wife on that movie, Raly Radouloff, the best call I ever made. She had worked on the film as a translator, and when I went back to do the sound mix in the Spring of 1991, my pal Davies had given me some letters to give Raly. I cannot say for sure that she received the letters, but I know that I received something I never cease to appreciate.

10

Later Then

Yes, we were disappointed (read: really bummed) that we didn't get renewed for a season three. Though in fact, they doubtless had all the material they would ever need. Anything that was photographed in Seasons One and Two could easily be re-voiced and changed into something else. Indeed, the show ran in reruns through the 70s without anything new being shot.

This, from the website, Internet Movie Data Base, IMDb, describes how the show was treated after its first run on Saturday mornings on NBC: Syndicated versions were cut down to half hour slots and renamed *The Banana Splits & Friends Show*. In this version, animated segments of *The Three Musketeers* and *Arabian Knights* would appear on alternate episodes (odds and evens respectively). *Danger Island* would also be cut down from 10mins to 5mins, with only the segments on the even-numbered episodes having the true cliff-hanger (the odd-numbered ones would sometimes stop at an appropriate moment or just end abruptly). *Micro Ventures* would also be slotted in if time permitted on select episodes in the latter part of the run. It was these episodes that were broadcast on Cartoon Network and released on DVD by Warner Guild Home Video, who had released four cassettes in the UK in the early 80s each featuring an omnibus of these editions, but without the *Danger Island* sequences.

There was one grand surprise remaining when the show was sold to other venues different from the original. That is, we were paid a buy-out fee. It was enough for me to go out and buy a very used Mercedes-Benz for about four thousand dollars. It was a beautiful 1960 220SE with a sunroof and nine, count 'em, **nine** glove compartments. Two years later I was broke and circled back to the guy from whom I'd bought the car and he gave me back what I'd paid for it. If I'd held onto it, it'd be worth well over 100,000 dollars now, with an equal amount of cost keeping it going, of course.

You can't look backwards and survive life with your nervous system intact. The "if only" game is hopeless and dreary. All any of us can do is press on. I know that's true for me. I went to USC to be a director and when I got out, I had no idea which foot to put in front of the other. I worked briefly as a film editor and wrote at night with my writing partner and old friend Alec Lorimore, and eventually we started selling our material and getting assignments from studios. Twelve years later, Julie Corman gave me a directing shot: Thanks, Julie, truly—and for twenty-plus years I cranked out movies and television. It's a minor miracle, I know that. I was allowed to apply what I studied at school. From what I can tell, this is a rare, rare gift.

My older brother Jeff went on to do many small acting bits in television and movies, but his main thrust was as a voice guy. He did scads of different voices, including the voice of the McDonald's French fries. He passed on in 2006 from a brain tumor and he is missed tremendously. Not a day goes by that I don't think of him. I cannot look at any of the material we did without being impressed by how hard Jeff was working it under all that chartreuse fur. He was so animated and inventive. He made the rest of look as if we were standing still.

My younger brother Dan never had the burning urge that Jeff and I did to be in the movie business. He quite wisely applied his mathematical prowess and went into being a computer programmer for the USGS (the United State Geological Survey.) They gave him all manner of training and flew him all over the country. Later in life, however, much later, he went down a path carved out by Larry Wachowski when he became Lana Wachowski. Dan decided that he'd had enough of being Dan Winkless and decided he'd be Anne Withrow (our mother's maiden name.) I can offer no particular insight on any level into his motivation for going down this road. I know only that he had it done in Thailand. I don't know what it cost. I don't know if there are any regrets about taking this action. The reason I don't know is that over the years we simply went such radically different directions in our lives that we aren't close enough to talk about anything tricky. So, I was not consulted about his transition, and do not wish to make this book a referendum or platform for discussing its efficacy. Different strokes for different folks. I did consult him about the piece you're reading and I didn't hear any disapproval.

Robert Towers has a list of credits as long as your arm, with everything from *Frasier* to *Hannah Montana,* to *Masters of the Universe* and *Will and Grace.* It's terrific getting together with him at these nostalgia/autograph events, especially after all this time.

Thanks to the stalwart efforts of Stuart Hersh, we have big line up of those events. We meet a lot of fans and shake a lot of hands. It's been a wild ride and all anybody can do is hold on, have fun, and hope it goes on and on.

– THW

Vancouver, BC, March, 2020

Post-Script

In February 2020, I returned from a second autograph/nostalgia event, this one in Burbank, California, and held at the Burbank Airport Marriott. Once again it was packed with people who were effusive in their joy for the show and the zany characters—why else come out? It's almost impossible to put into words how much fun it is knowing what great thrills people get out of coming out to meet us—and not just us of course; we were accompanied by a vast raft of celebrities, including Lorenzo Lamas, Branscomb Richmond, Ed Asner, Kelly Hu, Annabeth Gish, Johnny Crawford, among others, and former cast members of films and TV I directed: Alex Datcher, Marc Singer, and Brian Thompson, all of whom it was great seeing again and catching up with. There's a whole lot of hail-fellow-well-met at these events, and in a world as tense and divided as the one we inhabit, it's terrific to come together with people for a little while and forget all those striations. I'm sure I'm not alone in feeling this way; every so often you need to be in a room where at any moment somebody might burst into REM's "Shiny Happy People." As of this writing there's a rumor of additional shows in New York City, Lexington, Kentucky, Rhode Island, and Colorado. You don't have to twist my arm; my passport is ready, my bags packed. Bingo's wide, toothy grin has been good to me for a very long time; here's hoping he has made you grin just as widely a time or two over the decades.

* * *

I've had help reconstructing what happened when and owe some thank you acknowledgements—

So, big thanks go out to Steve Cox, Dan Ellithorpe, Scott Awley, and Robert Towers.

Index

www.ingramcontent.com/pod-product-compliance
Lightning Source LLC
LaVergne TN
LVHW010629100826
845148LV00014B/3166
9781629335643